PLANNER

ISBN: 979-8-8693-9266-4

THIS PLANNER BELONGS TO

____

____

Things to Remember

Important Dates

Books I want to Read

Movies I want to See

<table>
<tr><td>Places I want to Visit</td><td>Things that Inspire me</td></tr>
</table>

EVENTS

RANDOM IDEAS

Week of: _____________

MONDAY

TUESDAY

WEDNESDAY

Thursday

Friday

Saturday

Sunday

Week of: ___________

MONDAY

TUESDAY

WEDNESDAY

Thursday

Friday

Saturday

Sunday

Week of: _______________

MONDAY

TUESDAY

WEDNESDAY

> Opportunity is
> missed by most people
> because it is
> dressed in overalls
> and looks like work.
> ~Thomas Edison

Thursday

Friday

Saturday

Sunday

MONDAY

TUESDAY

WEDNESDAY

We must become the change we want to see.
~Mahatma Gandhi

THURSDAY

FRIDAY

SATURDAY

SUNDAY

Week of: _____________

MONDAY

TUESDAY

WEDNESDAY

Edison failed 10, 000 times before he made the electric light. Do not be discouraged if you fail a few times.

~Napoleon Hill

Thursday

Friday

Saturday

Sunday

Week of: ___________

MONDAY

....

....

....

....

....

....

....

TUESDAY

....

....

....

....

....

....

....

WEDNESDAY

....

....

....

....

....

....

If we did the things we are capable of, we would astound ourselves.
~Thomas A. Edison

Thursday

Friday

Saturday

Sunday

Week of: _____________

MONDAY

··
··
··
··
··
··
··

TUESDAY

··
··
··
··
··
··
··

WEDNESDAY

··
··
··
··
··

We can't help everyone, but everyone can help someone.
~Ronald Reagan

Thursday

Friday

Saturday

Sunday

Week of: _____________

MONDAY

TUESDAY

WEDNESDAY

Thursday

Friday

Saturday

Sunday

Week of: _______________

MONDAY

TUESDAY

WEDNESDAY

All our dreams
can come true -
if we have the courage
to pursue them.
~Walt Disney

Thursday

Friday

Saturday

Sunday

Week of: ___________

MONDAY

TUESDAY

WEDNESDAY

> *What great thing*
> *would you attempt*
> *if you knew*
> *you could not fail?*
> *~Robert H. Schuller*

THURSDAY

FRIDAY

SATURDAY

SUNDAY

Week of: _________

MONDAY

....

....

....

....

....

....

TUESDAY

....

....

....

....

....

....

WEDNESDAY

....

....

....

....

....

....

*When I let go
of what I am,
I become
what I might be.
~Lao Tzu*

Thursday

Friday

Saturday

Sunday

Week of: ___________

MONDAY

TUESDAY

WEDNESDAY

Thursday

Friday

Saturday

Sunday

Week of: _____________

MONDAY

TUESDAY

WEDNESDAY

*A loving heart
is the beginning
of all knowledge.
~Thomas Carlyle*

Thursday

Friday

Saturday

Sunday

Week of: ___________

MONDAY

TUESDAY

WEDNESDAY

Positive thinking will let you do everything better than negative thinking will.
~Zig Ziglar

Thursday

Friday

Saturday

Sunday

Week of: __________

MONDAY

TUESDAY

WEDNESDAY

*Every child
is an artist.
The problem is
how to remain an artist
once he grows up.
~Pablo Picasso*

Thursday

Friday

Saturday

Sunday

Week of: ___________

MONDAY

TUESDAY

WEDNESDAY

When people talk,
listen completely.
Most people never listen.
~Ernest Hemingway

Thursday

Friday

Saturday

Sunday

Week of: ___________

MONDAY

TUESDAY

WEDNESDAY

Thursday

Friday

Saturday

Sunday

Week of: _______________

MONDAY

TUESDAY

WEDNESDAY

Problems cannot be solved by the same level of thinking that created them.
~Albert Einstein

Thursday

Friday

Saturday

Sunday

Week of: _______________

MONDAY

TUESDAY

WEDNESDAY

Action is the foundational key to all success.
~Pablo Picasso

Thursday

Friday

Saturday

Sunday

Week of: _____________

MONDAY

TUESDAY

WEDNESDAY

*Love, you know,
seeks to make happy
rather than to be happy.
~Ralph Connor*

Thursday

Friday

Saturday

Sunday

Week of: ___________

MONDAY

TUESDAY

WEDNESDAY

> Do not
> dwell in the past,
> do not dream of the future,
> concentrate the mind
> on the present moment.
> ~Buddha

Thursday

Friday

Saturday

Sunday

Week of: _______________

MONDAY

TUESDAY

WEDNESDAY

Thursday

Friday

Saturday

Sunday

Week of: _____________

MONDAY

TUESDAY

WEDNESDAY

I have no special talents. I am only passionately curious.
~Albert Einstein

Thursday

Friday

Saturday

Sunday

Week of: _______________

MONDAY

TUESDAY

WEDNESDAY

*Creativity is
a natural extension
of our enthusiasm.
~Earl Nightingale*

THURSDAY

FRIDAY

SATURDAY

SUNDAY

Week of: ___________

MONDAY

TUESDAY

WEDNESDAY

> If we have the attitude that it is going to be a great day it usually is.
> ~Catherine Pulsife

Thursday

Friday

Saturday

Sunday

MONDAY

TUESDAY

WEDNESDAY

> *Most people
> are about as happy
> as they make up
> their minds to be.*
> *~Abraham Lincoln*

Thursday

Friday

Saturday

Sunday

Week of: _____________

MONDAY

··

··

··

··

··

··

··

TUESDAY

··

··

··

··

··

··

··

WEDNESDAY

··

··

··

··

··

··

*Success is the
sum of small efforts,
repeated day in
and day out.
~Robert Collier*

Thursday

Friday

Saturday

Sunday

Week of: _____________

MONDAY

TUESDAY

WEDNESDAY

All life
is an experiment.
The more experiments
you make the better.
~Ralph Waldo Emerson

Thursday

Friday

Saturday

Sunday

MONDAY

TUESDAY

WEDNESDAY

> The power of
> imagination
> makes us infinite.
> ~John Muir

Thursday

Friday

Saturday

Sunday

Week of: ___________

MONDAY

TUESDAY

WEDNESDAY

Worry is a misuse of imagination.
~Dan Zadra

Thursday

Friday

Saturday

Sunday

MONDAY

TUESDAY

WEDNESDAY

> *Idealism is what precedes experience, cynicism is what follows.*
> ~David T. Wolf

Thursday

Friday

Saturday

Sunday

MONDAY

TUESDAY

WEDNESDAY

*Oh for a book
and a shady nook...*
~John Wilson

Thursday

Friday

Saturday

Sunday

Week of: ___________

MONDAY

TUESDAY

WEDNESDAY

*There shall be
eternal summer in the
grateful heart.
~Celia Thaxter*

Thursday

Friday

Saturday

Sunday

MONDAY

TUESDAY

WEDNESDAY

> *I've never quite believed that one chance is all I get.*
> ~Anne Tyler

Thursday

Friday

Saturday

Sunday

MONDAY

TUESDAY

WEDNESDAY

If my hands are fully occupied

in holding on to something

I can neither give nor receive.

~Dorothee Solle

Thursday

Friday

Saturday

Sunday

MONDAY

TUESDAY

WEDNESDAY

*Life is like
an ever-shifting kaleidoscope -
a slight change
and all patterns alter.
~Sharon Salzberg*

THURSDAY

FRIDAY

SATURDAY

SUNDAY

WEEK OF: _______

MONDAY

TUESDAY

WEDNESDAY

Thursday

Friday

Saturday

Sunday

MONDAY

TUESDAY

WEDNESDAY

> The truly rich are those
> who enjoy what they have.
> ~Yiddish Proverb

Thursday

Friday

Saturday

Sunday

WEEK OF: _________

MONDAY

TUESDAY

WEDNESDAY

Thursday

Friday

Saturday

Sunday

Week of: _________

Monday

Tuesday

Wednesday

Every moment
is a fresh beginning.
~T.S. Eliot

Thursday

Friday

Saturday

Sunday

Week of: _____________

MONDAY

TUESDAY

WEDNESDAY

Thursday

Friday

Saturday

Sunday

MONDAY

TUESDAY

WEDNESDAY

> *Make each day your masterpiece.*
> ~John Wooden

Thursday

Friday

Saturday

Sunday

WEEK OF: __________

MONDAY

TUESDAY

WEDNESDAY

*Dwell on
the beauty of life.
Watch the stars,
and see yourself
running with them.
~Marcus Aurelius*

Thursday

Friday

Saturday

Sunday

MONDAY

TUESDAY

WEDNESDAY

Put your heart, mind, and soul into even your smallest acts. This is the secret of success.
~Swami Sivananda

Thursday

Friday

Saturday

Sunday

WEEK OF: _________

MONDAY

TUESDAY

WEDNESDAY

Thursday

Friday

Saturday

Sunday

WEEK OF: _____________

MONDAY

TUESDAY

WEDNESDAY

Strive not to be a success,
but rather to be of value.
~Albert Einstein

Thursday

Friday

Saturday

Sunday

MONDAY

TUESDAY

WEDNESDAY

Try to be a rainbow in someone's cloud.
~Maya Angelou

Thursday

Friday

Saturday

Sunday

WEEK OF: _________

MONDAY

TUESDAY

WEDNESDAY

No act of kindness,
no matter how small,
is ever wasted.

~Aesop

Thursday

Friday

Saturday

Sunday

MONDAY

TUESDAY

WEDNESDAY

> Keep your face
> always toward the sunshine
> and shadows
> will fall behind you.
> ~Walt Whitman

Thursday

Friday

Saturday

Sunday

WEEK OF: __________

MONDAY

TUESDAY

WEDNESDAY

Thursday

Friday

Saturday

Sunday

WEEK OF: _________

MONDAY

TUESDAY

WEDNESDAY

Thursday

Friday

Saturday

Sunday

MONDAY

TUESDAY

WEDNESDAY

*Be yourself
because an original
is always worth more
than a copy.
~Suzy Kassem*

Thursday

Friday

Saturday

Sunday

Do what you feel
in your heart to be right -
for you'll be criticized anyway.
~Eleanor Roosevelt

Notes

Notes

Let the beauty
of what you love
be what you do.
~Rumi

NOTES

NOTES

Do something wonderful,
people may imitate it.
~Albert Schweitzer

NOTES

NOTES

Rise above the storm and you will find the sunshine.
~Mario Fernández

Notes

Notes

Notes

Notes

Notes

Notes

NOTES

NOTES

"Write it on your heart
that every day
is the BEST day in the year."
-Ralph Waldo Emerson